Sleepwalking Beneath the Stars

by Howard Schwartz

Poetry
Vessels
Gathering the Sparks
Sleepwalking Beneath the Stars

Fiction
A Blessing Over Ashes
Midrashim
The Captive Soul of the Messiah
Rooms of the Soul

Editor
Imperial Messages: One Hundred Modern Parables
Voices Within the Ark: The Modern Jewish Poets
Gates to the New City: A Treasury of Modern Jewish Tales
Elijah's Violin & Other Jewish Fairy Tales
Miriam's Tambourine: Jewish Folktales from Around the World
Lilith's Cave: Jewish Tales of the Supernatural
The Dream Assembly: Tales of Rabbi Zalman Schachter-Shalomi

Children's Books
The Diamond Tree
The Sabbath Lion

BkMk Press

University of Missouri-Kansas City

SLEEPWALKING BENEATH THE STARS

Howard Schwartz

Illustrated by
John Brandi

ACKNOWLEDGMENTS

Some of these poems have previously been published in the following journals, to whose editors grateful acknowledgment is made: *Delmar, Minnesota Review, River Styx, The Sagarin Review, Sou'wester,* and *Studies in American Jewish Literature.*

Some of these poems have previously been published in the following anthology: *Five Missouri Poets* (Chariton Review Press).

Poems, Copyright © 1992 by Howard Schwartz

Illustrations, Copyright © 1992 by John Brandi

All Rights Reserved.

Library of Congress Cataloging-in-Publication Data
Schwartz, Howard, 1945-.
   Sleepwalking beneath the stars : poems / by Howard Schwartz
    p.   cm.
   ISBN 0-933532-82-2 : $9.50 cloth
   I. Title
PS3569.C5657S57   1991
   811'.54—dc20   91-26708
                                                                                      CIP

Financial assistance for this book has been provided by the Missouri Arts Council, a state agency.

Bk Mk Press brings readers the best in contemporary American poetry and international literature. A small literary press, unique among university publishers, Bk Mk ("Bookmark") Press operates under the aegis of the College of Arts and Sciences at the University of Missouri-Kansas City.

BkMk Press

Dan Jaffe, Director
Rae Furnish, Associate Editor

Typography, Book & Jacket Design by Michael Annis

IN MEMORY OF JAMES WRIGHT

*Between trees, a slender woman lifts up the lovely shadow
Of her face, and now she steps into the air, now she is gone
Wholly, into the air.*
— James Wright

I THE COVENANT OF THE STARS

Miriam's Well	10
The Scribe	11
Mermaids	12
The Covenant of the Stars	13
Going Back	14
Tree of Life	15
The Dark Orchard	16
Sleepwalking Beneath the Stars	17
A House	18
The Long Breath of the Black Swan	19

II THE KNOTTED FOREST

Dream Palm	22
The Stone Child	23
How My Pillar of Salt Is Wasted	24
Salt	25
Sisters	26
Guarding Against the Evil Eye	27
The Pit of Babel	28
Courting Oblivion	29
The Rag and Bone Shop	30
The Cave of the Four Winds	31
Braille Landscape	32
The Knotted Forest	33
City of the Dead	35
The Silver Tree	36
Tunisian Nights	37

THE WATERS OF OBLIVION	38
MEMORY OF THE FLOOD	39
LAILAH	40

III THE GUIDES

THE GUIDES	44
THE IBBUR	45
AN APPARITION	46
ORACLE OF THE OIL	47
SETTING THE TURTLES FREE	48
GHOSTS REHEARSING THE PAST	49
GIVING UP THE GHOST	50
THE GOLDEN DOVE	51
QUESTIONS FOR THE TALKING TREE	52
WIND CHIMES	53
THE BLACK DOLPHIN	54
A HANDFUL OF SCATTERED SPARKS	55
THE NINE FACES OF THE BRIDE	57

    1. The Spirit of the Wind
    2. The Lost Princess
    3. The Eternal Bride
    4. The Robe of the Shekhinah
    5. Her Mourning
    6. Her Exile
    7. The Sabbath Queen
    8. Song of Ascent
    9. Matronit

STRIKING THE ROCK	64

T H E   S T A R S

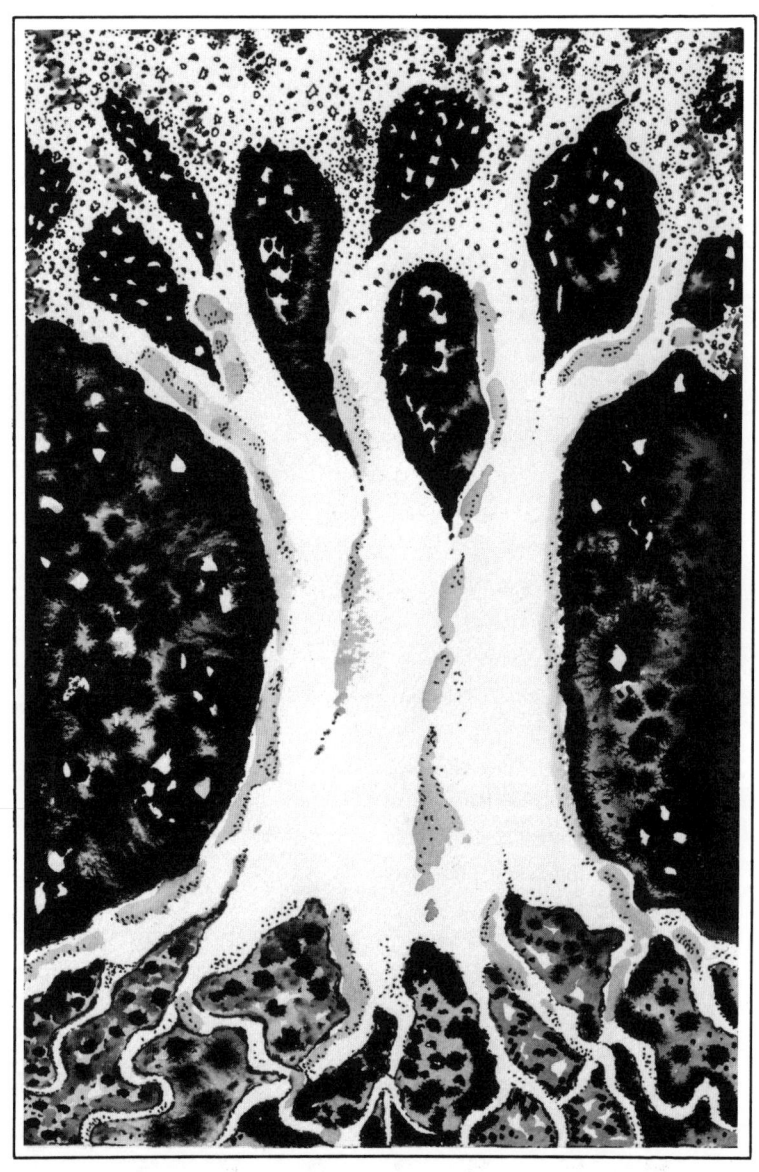

I

THE COVENANT OF THE STARS

> *Look now toward heaven,*
> *and count the stars,*
> *if you are able to.*
> *So shall be thy seed.*
> — Gen. 15:5

Miriam's Well

> *Every place our forefathers went,*
> *the well went before them.*
> —Pirke de Rabbi Eliezer

Her well
Wanders with me
Even when I am lost.

Not that I can always find it.

Yet it is always
Nearby
Like a golden dove
Buried beneath
The sand.

If only I could hold it in my hands
Surely
The heat would warm
Its wings
Surely
It would take
Flight—

If only
I could remember
My thirst
I would know where to look for it
With my eyes
Closed.

The Scribe

Even now
He is watching your life
Unfold
Recording every detail
Before it fades
Before the dark side takes root
Before the roots descend
To the cave
Of the forgotten
Sea.

Later
He will sift through everything
Casting days
And years
Into a black hole
Saving only a kernel
Ripe enough
To remember.

Mermaids

They are Pharaoh's children
Drowned
In the Red Sea
Old women
Banished
From the face of the earth.

They are spirits of the deep
Called forth
Daughters of the sea
And the sun
A race of dolphins
That mated with men.

Their sisters the sirens
Cry out to the waves
Embracing them
Gathering the souls
Of the drowned
Into their domain.

One of them always turns up
When you drift
In the Lost Sea —
Which one
Will it be
This time?

THE COVENANT OF THE STARS

I tried
To escape
The covenant of the sands
Every demand
Of destiny
Every shadow
Of the law
I hid
From the pillar of salt
By day
Ran from the pillar of fire
At night.

Still
The covenant of the stars
Beckoned
Each star
A seed taking root
A ripe dandelion
Waiting for the wind
A sensual stone
A tree breathing
Above the living
Waters.

Going Back

All night
The shadow of an ancient bird
Circled below me
Each turning taking me back
One year
At a time.

Back
Until it was time to be
Reborn
Back even further
Until all I could remember
Was how a seed
Grows ripe.

Back
To the instant
I was conceived
Looking down from the door
Of the seed
At spinning planets of light
Rising up
From below.

Still
The ancient bird
Circled
But I knew
If I went back
Any further
I might not be able
To return.

Tree of Life

The smallest branches
Break off
On their own
And come alive
Crawling toward the dark
Waters
Soon
There are clusters
Of tiny fish
Filling the depths
A shimmering cloud
Rising up
From below
Breaking free of the waters
A flock
Of sparrows
Taking flight.

The Dark Orchard

Better to sail on an unknown sea
Than to become lost
In that garden
Of forking
Paths.

One
Who entered there
Looked
And died
One looked
And lost his mind
One cut the shoots
Cutting himself
Off
Only one
Entered
And departed
In peace.

Those
Who wander there
Know there is no exit
Only a caravan
Of spirits
All those who have gone before us
In search
Of light.

Sleepwalking Beneath the Stars

She seems to float
No higher than a hand's breadth
Across the field
Somehow
She knows exactly where she is going
As if her eyes were open
As if a falling star had imprinted itself
On her palm
As if her palm were a map of the orchard
She has entered
A braille landscape
Waiting to be
Read.

By now
You know it would be dangerous
To wake her
Who knows
What small roots would never recover
What shoots would never begin
To grow
Still
Even the slightest wind
Threatens to carry her off
Her frail image almost lost in the darkness
As she passes between
The trees.

Even now
The dark stars hide their light
And every blossom holds its breath
For if the plague of darkness lasts much longer
She too may be enslaved by silence
And never emerge from the orchard
In peace.

A House

This house
Can only be explored
At night
As you slowly descend
The stairway
Into sleep.

The roof is a firmament
Of stars
The cellar
A dark sea
Every window looks out
On another land.

No one owns
Or can own
This house
Those who live there
Are only passing
Through.

THE LONG BREATH OF THE BLACK SWAN

She was once as familiar and mutable as the moon
Gathering tides at nightfall
Searching for the sea hidden inside the dark
Shell.

Night after night
We crossed the ocean back and forth
Rowing on the waters with arms of air.

Adrift in the starlight
We heard the oracle of the deep
The long breath of the black swan
The rising and falling of the moontide
That swept us away.

Once she made her home here
Now I search for her in every shadow
In every pocket of memory
I close my eyes
And search for her
Within.

II
THE KNOTTED FOREST

And it came to pass,
when the sun was going down,
a deep sleep fell upon him,
lo, a dread, even a great darkness.
— Gen. 15:12

DREAM PALM

The right has memorized
Ancient histories,
Entrances and exits,
Angles of repose
And abandoned maps.
Someday its lifeline will serve
As a death-mask.

But the left—
All its coastlines are uncharted.
Like the room in my mother's dream
No one enters,
Its clay is incomplete,
An eyeless needle
Sworn to silence.

The Stone Child

She has carried the child
So long
It has turned to stone
Still
It has retained
A faint pulse
Even as the dim sea
Turns to sand.

Once it was rocking
In its cradle
Exploring the face
Of every ancestor
Every birth
And death—
Now it only weighs her
Down.

As for the child
It is still waiting
To be born.

How My Pillar of Salt Is Wasted

One by one
The grains slip away
Beneath my feet.

The shadow of the sun
Grows shorter.

When I awake
The sound of gnawing
Lays bare its desperate pulse
Like the rush of falls.

Soon it becomes
My silence.

Salt

—for Harry Weber

Salt
Became so scarce
It was worth its weight in gold.
Not only the shelves
Were empty:
The salt
Had even vanished
From the sea.

What little
Was left
We hoarded.
Too soon
Even the hoards
Were empty.

We dug in the earth
Everywhere
Searching for salt.
But it had all
Disappeared.

Salt was more precious
Than the veins in which
It flowed.
They were willing to kill
For it.

I have a little salt left.
I am afraid
They will try to take it
Away.

Sisters

One sister chases the night
Wherever it goes
Slipping
Beneath doors
Like a shadow
Between
The cracks
Under
The sheets.

Her name is known by all
Spoken
By none.

Her sister
Queen
Of the seventh day
Was first conceived
As a blessing
As a seed
Of light
Spiraling into
Being.

After all these years
Her name is still
Unknown.

GUARDING AGAINST THE EVIL EYE

Lilith turns away
From the eye that is always open
From the hand that holds her back
Fettered by the ancient vow
She crawls back
Into her cave
Coiled inside
The roots
Of dreams.

But surely she will be back
Bearing the shadow
Of the unborn
As the planet spins
Towards the dark
Sea.

All you can do
Is call upon the guardian
The eye in the hand that sees in the dark
Feeling the way
Through this cavern
One step
At a time.

The Pit of Babel

In your wanderings
You may have stumbled
On the Pit of Babel
The mouth
Of the abyss
The faultline
Always ready
To crack.

Even now
You may be standing
On it.

Courting Oblivion

Come here
She says
Dancing on the edge
Flicking one rose petal
After another
Into the abyss.

And every hour
You move one step
Closer
Your eyes fixed
On the breast
That has almost torn free
From her gown
Averted from the other
Dry as a raisin
From which she suckles
Death.

But which one will she offer?

Come here
She whispers
Crooking her finger
Swaying her hips
Come closer.

THE RAG AND BONE SHOP

The finest clothes turn to rags.
Be careful all day long.
— I Ching

Perhaps
You expect to find it
In the cellar
Behind the locked door
No
It is not there.

Not in a dark cave
Not in a dry well
Not in a field or forest
Not in an orchard or garden
Not in a blessing
Not in a curse
Not on the first day
Not on the last.

Not in the feast
Not in the famine
Not in the planting
Not in the growing ripe
Not in all you can remember
Not in all you would
Forget.

Not in the East
Not in the West
Not in Limbo
Not in the Promised Land
Not at the end of the rainbow
Not at the end of the road.

Not in the stars
Not in the grave
Not in the rags
Not in the bones
Not here
Not yet.

THE CAVE OF THE FOUR WINDS

The cave of the four winds
Is covered by a curtain
If only a corner
Is lifted
The winds
Will bring down a rain
Of blessings.

But pull the curtain
Apart
And the covenant of being
Will be broken
The breath will be torn
From every body
The world will return
To chaos.

In the cave
Behind the curtain
Even the winds
Hold their breath.

BRAILLE LANDSCAPE

Nothing was left him
but touch
— Zbigniew Herbert

Not even the cave
Of your dreams
Is this dark.

Somehow
You must make your way
Until the letters hidden
In the ceiling
And walls
Flock into
Your hands.

Only then
Will the shapes
Shimmer
Like the oracle
Of the oil
Poured in Babylon
To read in the book
Of what has not yet been
Revealed.

Only then
Will the words rise up
On their own
Bearing a voice
You once knew so well—

How is it
That it has been lost to you
So long?

THE KNOTTED FOREST

In your travels
You too may become lost
In the knotted forest
Where the branches are so entangled
Nothing
Can loosen
The knot.

As you stumble in darkness
A star
Taking root in the branches
Will guide you to a small hut
Inside
You will see nothing but shelves
Each filled with a constellation
Of candles
One
For every one
Of us.

Know
That the old man
Who lets you in
Will answer
Only one question
Only one candle
Will be
Revealed.

If your candle
Is ablaze
Go back
With his blessings
If your candle

Is burning
Low
The valley of the shadow
Beckons
Keep repeating the prayer
For the living
Above all
Do not disturb
Any other
Flame.

If you do
Every sign of the hut
Will vanish
As well as the forest
And you will be a wanderer
In one of the forgotten
Worlds.

CITY OF THE DEAD

In Memory of Rabbi Arnold Asher

The road I took in that city
Was round
It was said
That all who started out
On that road
Would one day meet
All the others
Who followed
Its path.

I was searching
For you —
At the same time
I was afraid
I would find you.

THE SILVER TREE

In his dream
My father saw a silver tree
That had taken root
Outside his window.
He opened the door
And stepped out into the silver
Shadow.
Nor did he ever come back.

All those years
Spent in the study
Of silver
Learning what is precious,
What is not.

And now
Leaves beaten of the purest
Silver
With words inscribed
On every
Page.

TUNISIAN NIGHTS

All I caught
Were the final strains
Too fleeting
To grasp
Like the last scent of my father
On his pillow
After they carried him out.

All absences
Flow together
Into one wound.

We too shall be forgotten.

The Waters of Oblivion

Consider how much passes through our hands
Winds that reach us from southern shores
Swirling waters
Flocks of unseen birds—

That is why
Whatever feathers we find
When the whirlwind has passed
Are so precious.

So much abundance
So much absence
So long
To sip
The waters
As they
Evaporate.

Memory of the Flood

There was only
A single candle
Left
I closed my eyes
And tried to remember
The sun
A fine spray blew lightly across
My face
I lay back
As the last of a wave
Washed into the room
A great clap announced
Another wave
Water rose
And rocked the bed
An ark at sea.

Lailah

for Laya Firestone-Seghi

When the moon has grown ripe
Enough
She brings forth
Your wandering
Soul
And commands it
To enter
The seed.

Midwife
Of souls
She watches over you
And by the light that shines
Within
Reads
The long history of your soul
From the book of dreams.

Sometimes
You remember her
Whispering
In the dark
Until the history
Is imprinted
On every cell.

Sometimes
You hear her voice
Just before waking
Guiding your soul
As it threads its way
Back.

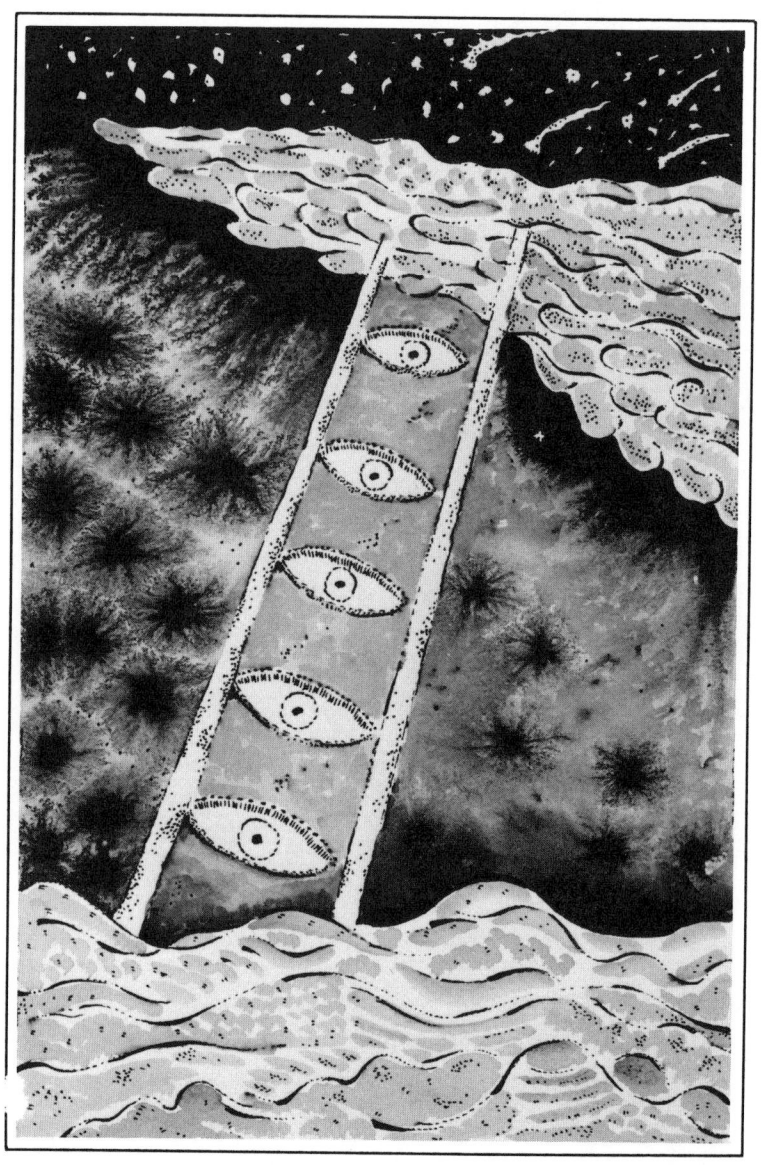

III
THE GUIDES

And he sent forth a dove.
— Gen. 8:8

THE GUIDES

Two fathers
Guide me
Wherever I go.

One
Will never abandon me
The other
Has escaped
From the tomb
To be here.

Even now
They are waiting for me
To follow.

THE IBBUR

> *The soul of an ancestor or a master may, in order to comfort or instruct, enter into the soul of someone who has suffered misfortune. Ibbur is the name given to this variety of metempsychosis.*
> — Jorge Luis Borges

He has come a great distance
Carried like a comet through stars scattered
Like broken vessels
Drawn by the fire that descends
To consume
The offering.

Whether you know it
Or not
You have called him
Forth.

His soul
Descends to you
By the ladder of dreams
When you awake
You will be
One.

An Apparition

All at once
The forest that would not reveal
A single path
Opens before you
A space in the leaves
In the shape of an ethereal body
That beckons
Guiding you
Into the vine-covered valley
Where a stream of light pours forth
From the tree of blessings
Each wind bearing its own blessing
To the far corners
Of creation
Taking root
Above
And below.

ORACLE OF THE OIL

When every shadow and every echo
Have disappeared
Pour a little oil
Into the hollow of your hand
Enough to form a small mirror
Soon
Worlds will come into being
And disappear
A sea
Of stars
Taking root in your hand.

Look closely
Before the mirror grows dark
If you can see the face
Of the full moon
You will be blessed
If all you can see is a circle
You will wander in exile
Until it is time
To return
If the mirror has grown
Dark
Close your eyes
Before it is too late
And consult the seer
Within.

Setting the Turtles Free

for Shira and Nathan

All summer
We watched
As they huddled together
Or drifted apart
At night
Their images crawled into
Our dreams
Multiplying.

On the last day
Of summer
We took them to the forest
Wandering away from the path
Until we ourselves
Were lost
And there
We let them go.

They left three eggs
Planted
In the earth —
Who knows what
Will break out
Of those hard
Shells?

Ghosts Rehearsing the Past

Waking at night
Another dream world
Abandoned
The last images
Swirling through my fingers
Like sand
The darkness
Indecipherable
All the mirrors grown
Dark.

In that dark
Reflection
I see myself
Surrounded by shadows
All I have forgotten
Ghosts rehearsing
The past.

Even now
The family is gathering
All the voices lost
In mourning
Whispers
So faint
Not even a dream
Remembers.

Giving Up the Ghost

For years she accompanied me
Everywhere
I held the torch for her
While she danced her shadow dance
And I watched
Hypnotized
As the years
Passed.

Sometimes
I saw her face to face
Sometimes
Her face was turned away
Yet her shadow
Still mingled
With mine
Sometimes
I imagined
She had disappeared
But she always came back
To haunt me
Faithful
In her absence
Even then
We were inseparable.

Now
As I bid her
Farewell
I find her sleepwalking
In her funeral veil —
The same one she wore
As a bride —
And I know

At last
That I can give up
The ghost.

THE GOLDEN DOVE

Sister
Of the voice
The song of the golden dove
Echoes
From an unseen
Nest
Could I hear her so clearly
If the gates were not
Open?

Once
She was only an arm's reach
Away
If the ladder
Of prayers
Had not fallen
I might have brought her
Back.

Still
Even if she did elude me
I was blessed to hear
Her song
Once
During this season
Where silence has taken
Root.

Questions for the Talking Tree

How much
Has been held back?

Only the rain knows.

How much
Remains?

A single star at the center
Enough to get
Your bearings

Where
Should I look for her now?

Where the veil that hangs
Before everything
Is lifted.

Where is the song
Concealed?

Where the dancer sings
Herself
Voice and quivering reed
And the dance
Falls from her
As sound
From a humming
Gong.

Wind Chimes

They play
When the spirit moves them
Rousing you.

Somewhere
The moon has not been eclipsed
Somewhere
There are stars left to count.

Even now
The wind draws its breath
Back and forth
Inventing this music
For the first time

And the last.

THE BLACK DOLPHIN

for Donald Finkel

There is a black dolphin
Swimming in the same waters
With us
If you submerge
You will hear its song
Rising up
From within.

Yes
The dolphin is diving
Below.

Even now
It is searching
In the deep
For new songs
Each one another pearl
Recovered
From the waters
Of oblivion.

What other purpose do we serve
But to build a barrier
Against eternity
A fragile coral reef
Of song?

A Handful of Scattered Sparks

First
You must find
A handful
Of scattered sparks.

Know
That they could be
Anywhere
Disguised
As fallen stars:
Under the dark side of a leaf
In a hollow shell
Or glimmering
In a dark
Pool.

Too often
You return
With an empty sack
Slung over your shoulder.
This time
Bring back
A netful
Of scattered sparks.

Take them out
Hold them
In your hands.

Remember
How to contain
Them
How to keep them
From igniting

Until they are
Ripe.

Keep your hands closed
Like a cauldron
Wait
Until you can see
With the eye in your hand
A vision
Of the broken vessels
Still scattering
Their sparks.

When the sparks begin to throb
Like a golden bird
Starting to stir
Let go
Set them free
Scatter them all over
Again.

Let someone else
Find them.

The Nine Faces of the Bride

1. The Spirit of the Wind

Where the light
Of the first day
Still clings
To the shells of the broken
Vessels
The spirit of the wind
Still bears
The voice
That brought it
Into being.

No sooner
Have you named her
Than she begins
To speak.

Fire is always her first word
Then water
Out of these
Worlds can be created.

2. The Lost Princess

She lives
In exile
In a palace of pearls
Her face hidden
From every mirror
Still
You search for her
Everywhere
Letting the dead
Of the desert

Guide you
To the golden dove
Waiting for the wind
To reveal
The way
To the golden mountain
Where the lost princess
Waits.

3. The Eternal Bride

At midnight
The gate of the orchard
Opens
And you find her
Slowly taking form
Beside the falls
Her face
The face of your ancestors
Before they were born.

Each time she opens her eyes
Her song
Lost for so long
Returns
From its journey
Through the stars.

Even so
If you listen closely
You can hear
Her words
Recalling
The rain
Falling through branches
Yet to be

Carved
Drawing down a rain
Of blessings.

4. The Robe of the Shekhinah

She is the one who hovers
Over the flames
Of the parchment
So long
A spark catches
The hem of her robe
And it begins to burn—
Only when all the letters
Have taken flight
Does she rise up
After them
Illuminating
The night.

And from all that remains of the robe
A single
Thread
She weaves
Another garment
On the loom that stretches
From heaven
To earth
And each stitch she takes
Turns in a circle
That draws the worlds
Closer.

5. Her Mourning

Once
When the walls
Were unbroken
She was a bride in white
Now
Dressed in mourning
She tries to fill the cup
Of her empty hands.

Grief
Leads her
Through many mirrors
To seek you in the underworld
Bells chime slowly
As she descends the stairway
Into sleep.

There
She takes all the griefs saved up
So long
Each one an unspoken psalm
And gives every grief
A voice
Of its own
So that your soul might ascend
Another rung.

6. Her Exile

She follows
Every wandering
Path
Every thread
As it passes through

The eye
Of fate
Guiding her children
Through the rivers
Of darkness
The underground caves
The labyrinth
Of shattered
Vessels.

She follows
Every fire-cracked
Shell
Every broken
Branch
Every wind
That beckons
Every oracle
Waiting to be read
Searching for the river
Of scattered
Sparks
That will finally quench
Her thirst.

7. The Sabbath Queen

For six days
She wanders
In secret
Her light hidden
In a dark
Shell
Only on the seventh
Does her exile
Come to an end.

That is when
She gathers
The golden threads
Of the sun
Weaving the Sabbath songs
Into a garland
Of prayers
Into a crown
Of blessings
Into a tabernacle
Of peace.

8. Song of Ascent

She gathers the sparks
No matter how far they have flown
From the fire
Searching in every crevice
Under the dark side of every leaf
With each one she recovers
A fallen star
Once a sun in itself
Still glowing
Where the wings of the black swan
Repeat to the fire of the phoenix
The secrets of ascent:
How to rise up from your resting place
How to carry your cargo of light
How to break open like a blossom
At every turning of the spiral
Coiled inside
The permutations
Of the flame.

9. Matronit

Standing
On the narrow bridge
Between worlds
She speaks to you from behind
The curtain

That is where
She plants
The blessings
You bring her

And harvests
Their fire
Within.

STRIKING THE ROCK

The first time Moses struck the rock
Water began
To flow.

The second time
Songs poured out
Like a vessel being emptied
Of all that had grown
Ripe.

The third time
Angels crawled out
From where they had been sleeping
Forty centuries.

The fourth time
Moses glimpsed the face
Of the Messiah
Standing inside
A garden

And the gate
Was open.